101
OFFENSIVE LINE
DRILLS

Steve Loney

ISBN: 1-58518-258-3
Library of Congress Catalog Card Number: 00-108320

Book design and diagrams: Jeanne Hamilton
Cover design: Paul Lewis

Coaches Choice
P.O. Box 1828
Monterey, CA 93942
www.coacheschoice.com

DEDICATION

Through the highs and lows of my career, one thing has been a constant — the support and love from my wife of twenty-five years, Terri, and the unconditional love from my three children — Matt, Katie and Kylan. They are my greatest accomplishment.

To these four, I dedicate my efforts on this book.

ACKNOWLEDGMENTS

We are all a product of our environment and I am no different. As I view my career, my philosophies and my character, I look to several people that I owe a great deal of thanks and credit for any and all successes that I have enjoyed in my life.

My thanks goes out to my parents, Curt and Joan Loney, for without their efforts, I wouldn't have the grasp of right and wrong. Grant Peterson, Bill Barton, George Funk and George Haws, my junior and senior high school coaches in various sports, taught me that sports should be fun, but that you have to play hard and compete to win. My college coach and mentor, Earle Bruce, taught me the importance of hard work, being a great teacher and demanding more than the mind thinks is possible. Tom Lichtenberg, my closest friend in this profession, provided me with a great example of how to treat people and get close to players. Joe Bugel, for whom I worked in Phoenix, taught me a great deal about offensive line play. I must also add the following names to this list — Tom Moore, Sonny Moran, Rob Hicklin, Johnny Majors, Skip Holtz, Dan McCarney and Glen Mason, all of whom gave me a chance. I can only hope that I was never a disappointment to them.

Finally, my thanks goes to the many assistants with whom I have had the honor of working. I was influenced by them all.

CONTENTS

Steve Loney is one of the most respected offensive line coaches in the country today. Steve is known as a great fundamentalist, teacher and a man of detail. Nothing is ever left to chance. He works hard and demands the same of his players, keeping them always pointed in the right direction. No detail is too small. Steve believes that if you improve the individual, you will improve the team. He works hard with each individual - their problems are his problems. Steve has always given the players a thorough understanding and knowledge of their duties and responsibilities. He is a tremendous competitor and motivator. His players always give their all in each game.

I have known Steve Loney as a player, an assistant coach and offensive coordinator. I am more than pleased to call him a friend and introduce you to his book, "101 Offensive Line Drills". I would say that all coaches should possess this book — it is a great teaching tool.

Earle Bruce
Former Head Football Coach
Tampa, Iowa State, Ohio State,
Northern Iowa and Colorado State

PREFACE

The HEART AND SOUL of any football team is its OFFENSIVE LINE. No position in football requires more DISCIPLINE AND TECHNIQUE than in being an offensive lineman. The success of your offensive football team hinges on your ability to control the line of scrimmage. To win a conference championship, you *must* win in the trenches, and that means playing on your opponent's side of the line.

My approach up front will be to out-execute and out-effort our opponents. To take this approach and to believe in this philosophy means a great deal of time must be spent on blocking technique.

I have compiled the enclosed set of *101 Offensive Line Drills* from the drills that I have used over my more than two decades of coaching at the high school, college and professional levels. I have learned and borrowed these drills from many fine offensive line coaches and adapted each drill to the scheme and techniques that fit our offense.

I have taken the total development of the lineman from the off-season to agility to pass protection and finally to run blocking. I hope that this book helps each of you develop an offensive front of which you will be proud.

S.L.

CHAPTER 1

OFF-SEASON DEVELOPMENTAL DRILLS

DRILL #1: BIG BAG SETS

Objective: To develop the quickness of the set, body weight distribution, length and quickness of the punch, power and extension of the punch.

Equipment Needed: Hanging heavy bag.

Description: The lineman begins in his stance; his partner holds the big bag back and gives the cadence command. On the snap count, the lineman shoots back into his pass set, pulling his pads from the L.O.S., putting his pads and chest perpendicular to the ground, and lowering his hips, while holding his weight back with weight properly distributed on the inside of the legs. The partner varies when the bag is propelled at the lineman. On the snap count, he sends the bag toward the lineman at times and then changes up by pump faking to see if the lineman lunges forward. This drill is excellent for developing the timing involved in the punch.

Coaching Points:

- The lineman's hands should strike all punches with the heel of his hand, not his full hand.
- The hands should form a "W" with the thumbs pointing upward.
- Elbows are tight.
- The punch should be well-timed and should snap the bag back toward the partner.

DRILL #2: BIG BAG SETS WITH POWER STEPS

Objective: To place further emphasis on the lineman's set and body demeanor, with an additonal variable of requiring the lineman to shut down all inside moves.

Equipment Needed: Hanging heavy bag.

Description: The previous drill is repeated, except for the additional variable of having the lineman react to his partner occasionally sliding the bag to the lineman's inside.

Coaching Point:

• The offensive player must emphasize the power step flat down the L.O.S., while executing the proper punch.

DRILL #3: MEDICINE BALL SETS

Objective: To develop the ability of a lineman to punch with power and strength.

Equipment Needed: Medicine ball.

Description: The lineman assumes a proper stance with a medicine ball on the ground directly in front of him. On command, the player takes his set while grabbing the ball and driving it up to his partner.

Coaching Points:

- Keep in mind, the player should not bring the ball to his chest.
- Any arm extension should come from a slight bend in his elbows which are held in within the frame of the body.

 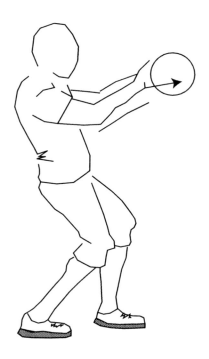

DRILL #4: MEDICINE BALL PUNCHES

Objective: To develop the lineman's timing of his punch.

Equipment Needed: Medicine ball.

Description: The lineman assumes a proper stance and takes a proper pass set upon the cadence command. His partner then lobs the ball to him. He then punches the ball back to the partner.

Coaching Points:

- The lineman should punch strike with the heels of his hand.
- It should be emphasized that the lineman should not draw his hands back to his chest.
- His arm extension should originate from a slight bend in each arm not exceeding a ninety-degree bend.

DRILL #5: MEDICINE BALL BENCH PRESS PUNCH

Objective: To work on the mechanics of the timing of each punch and the violence of the punch.

Equipment Needed: A medicine ball; a weight bench (optional).

Description: The lineman lies on his back with his partner standing next to his head. The partner starts the drill by tossing the ball to the chest of the lineman. The lineman has his arms extended with a slight bend in them, with his elbows tight to the body. The lineman punches the ball back to his partner, timing his explosion to snap the ball back.

Coaching Point:

•   It is important that the lineman does not draw the ball back to his chest, but rather explodes through the ball in order to snap it back to his partner.

DRILL #6: WEIGHTED PUNCHES

Objective: To teach the lineman proper body positioning while moving his feet using proper footwork; to condition the lineman by overloading his shoulder muscles.

Equipment Needed: A weight bar, a sand bag, or dumbbells.

Description: The lineman assumes a proper pass protection stance with the weighted object extended away from his body with a slight bend in his arms. On the snap count, the lineman takes a power step with his inside foot flat down the L.O.S., while thrusting his arms forward in order to simulate a punch. The lineman then retracts his weight as he retreats with the outside foot, again punching with each step. The drill continues with a power step, punch, kick, punch.

Coaching Point:

• The emphasis is on proper footwork, knee bend, and punch mechanics.

DRILL #7: SQUAT SHUTTLE

Objective: To emphasize the similarity between resistance exercise squats performed in a weight room and the proper body positioning involved in a good pass protection set.

Equipment Needed: A weight bar.

Description: The lineman begins in a good pass protection stance. On the snap count, the lineman power steps with his inside foot and slides with his trail foot. His feet do not come together as trail foot closes. His feet should always remain outside his hips. He arches his lower back while maintaining proper angles in his hips, knees and ankles. His shoulders remain back, slightly behind his knees, his chest is forward, and his chin is slightly down. He shuffles laterally in a 8-yard area back and forth.

Coaching Point:

• The drill should be executed with perfect body positioning.

DRILL #8: STICK DRILL

Objective: To teach the offensive blocker how to extend his outside arm on a reach block to get the defender's shoulder turned.

Equipment Needed: A broom stick.

Description: The players face each other, with a 90-degree bend in their arms. On the whistle, each player works to extend his outside arm to a lock-out position, while moving his outside foot downfield.

Coaching Point:

*   Strength in arm extension, quickness, body placement, and leverage are emphasized throughout this drill.

DRILL #9: QUARTER EAGLE

Objective: To teach quick movement while maintaining a good football position and correct weight distribution.

Equipment Needed: None.

Description: From a two-point stance, the linemen turn about an eighth of a turn to the right, then back to center, left, center, right, etc. Players turn sharply, keeping their feet on the ground, and pivoting in place. They turn on a visual signal from the coach. The drill is completed by having the players sprint forward for five yards on a visual signal from the coach.

Coaching Points:

- The players maintain a good football position with their weight distributed on the inside of legs and feet.
- Players should not be allowed to hop when moving.
- Keeping cleats in the ground as much as possible should be emphasized.

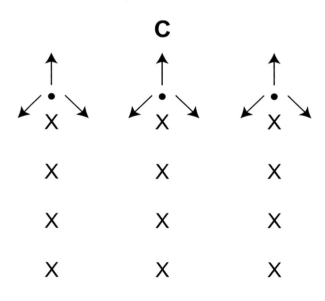

DRILL #10: TENNIS BALL

Objective: To develop the footwork involved in shuffling, while maintaining a good base with the knees bent; to develop quickness; to enhance stamina.

Equipment Needed: Four tennis balls.

Description: The coach faces the player who is in a good pass protection set. The coach rolls a ball to one side of the lineman. The player shuffles over in front of the ball and scoops it back to the coach who has rolled a second ball to which the player must react. The drill is performed continuously for a 20-second period of time.

Coaching Points:

- As the players become more skilled, the coach can speed the drill up.
- It should be emphasized to the lineman to get over in front of the ball as quickly as possible and to bend at his knees, not the waist.

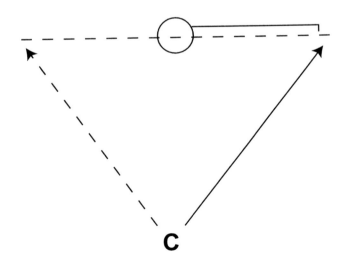

DRILL #11: ROPE SKIPPING — BASIC PROCEDURES

Objective: To develop the ability to skip rope properly; to enhance footwork, coordination, body awareness, and balance.

Equipment Needed: Jump rope.

Description: In order to jump rope properly, a lineman must be able to perform certain skills correctly, particulary turning the rope. For example, when turning the rope, the upper arms should be held close to the body. The forearms should be held down and out at a 45-degree angle with the hands 8-to-10 inches from the hips. In using a rope without hand grips, the rope should be grasped with the thumb and the second joint of the forefinger about four inches from the end, letting the remaining part rest loosely in the other three fingers. The hands should do most of the work in turning the rope. The hands should circumscribe a circle of six-to-eight inches. The arm movements should be cut down as much as possible except in those maneuvers that require greater arm action. Using this body position, the lineman should start bouncing without the rope, using a single-bounce movement. The tempo for this fundamental activity should be about 125 bounces per minute. Performing the drill should involve adhering to the following guidelines:

- Bounce one inch off the floor.
- Land slightly on the balls of the feet.
- Bend slightly at the ankles, knees and hips.
- Do at least 20-25 bounces.
- Rest for several seconds, resume the action and repeat this procedure three times.

Coaching Points:
- Initially, each of the skills involved in Drills #12-20 should be practiced at a relatively slow tempo and then stepped up once the lineman gets the feel of it.
- The following guidelines can be used to gauge how fast an individual is skipping: slow (125-130 turns per minute); medium (135-145); fast (150-160); and speed skipping (165-180).

DRILL #12: ROPE SKIPPING – SINGLE BOUNCE OR JUMP

Objective: To develop footwork, coordination, and balance.

Equipment Needed: Jump rope.

Description: With both feet together, the lineman bounces only once to each turn of the rope.

Coaching Point:

- The emphasis should be upon intense concentration, precision of movement, timing, and developing a high degree of the motor skills involved in skipping rope.

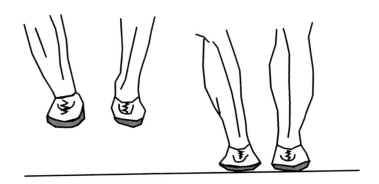

DRILL #13: ROPE SKIPPING — FORWARD/BACKWARD

Objective: To develop footwork, coordination, and balance.

Equipment Needed: Jump rope.

Description: The lineman alternately moves his feet forward and backward — his right foot forward and his left foot backward for the first turn of the rope, his left foot forward and his right foot backward for the next turn of the rope, etc. He should not return to the basic rope skipping position (i.e., feet side-by-side) in this maneuver.

Coaching Point:

*   The emphasis should be upon intense concentration, precision of movement, timing, and developing a high degree of the motor skills involved in skipping rope.

DRILL #14: ROPE SKIPPING – STRADDLE

Objective: To develop footwork, coordination, and balance.

Equipment Needed: Jump rope.

Description: The drill involves having the lineman return to the basic rope skipping position from a predetermined foot placement, for example, his feet are together on the one count, his feet spread on the two count, and his feet come back together on the three count.

Coaching Point:

* The emphasis should be upon intense concentration, precision of movement, timing, and developing a high degree of the motor skills involved in skipping rope.

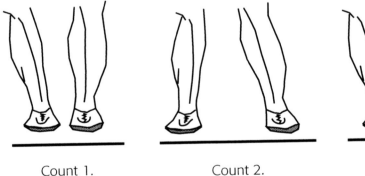

Count 1.   Count 2.   Count 3.

DRILL #15: ROPE SKIPPING— CRISSCROSS

Objective: To develop footwork, coordination, and balance.

Equipment Needed: Jump rope.

Description: Jumping rope, the lineman's arms are crossed at the elbows on the downward swing of the rope, jumping through the loop formed in front of his body. He then uncrosses his arms on the next downward swing of the rope.

Coaching Points:

- The emphasis should be upon intense concentration, precision of movement, timing, and developing a high degree of the motor skills involved in skipping rope.
- If the lineman's arms are crossed at the wrists, a small loop will result, making it difficult to jump through.

DRILL #16: ROPE SKIPPING – CROSS LEG

Objective: To develop footwork, coordination, and balance.

Equipment Needed: Jump rope.

Description: The drill involves having the lineman skip rope, while performing the following skipping sequence:

- A single bounce.
- Touch his right heel out in front as he does a left-foot bounce.
- Cross his right foot to his left in front of the bouncing foot, touching his toe to the floor.
- Touch his right heel out in front.
- Continue to repeat the procedure while alternating right- and left-foot bouncing.

Coaching Point:

- The emphasis should be upon intense concentration, precision of movement, timing, and developing a high degree of the motor skills involved in skipping rope.

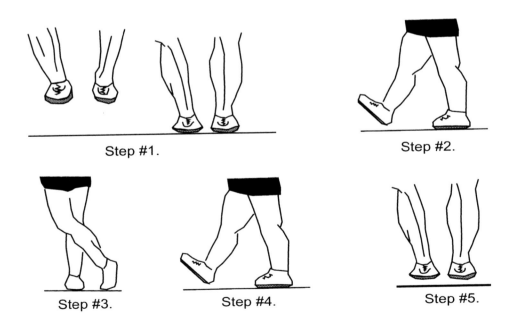

Step #1.　Step #2.　Step #3.　Step #4.　Step #5.

DRILL #17: ROPE SKIPPING — SINGLE SIDEWARD SPREAD

Objective: To develop footwork, coordination, and balance.

Equipment Needed: Jump rope.

Description: The drill involves having the lineman skip rope, while performing the following skipping sequence:

- A single bounce.
- As the lineman does a left-foot bounce, he should spread his right leg sideward, touching his foot to the floor 14-16 inches from the bouncing foot.
- Repeat the procedure while alternating right- and left-leg spreading out.

Coaching Point:

- The emphasis should be upon intense concentration, precision of movement, timing, and developing a high degree of the motor skills involved in skipping rope.

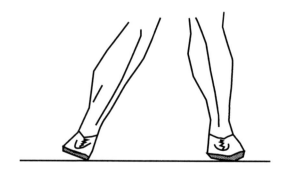

DRILL #18: ROPE SKIPPING — ROCKER

Objective: To develop footwork, coordination, and balance.

Equipment Needed: Jump rope.

Description: The drill involves having the lineman skip rope, while performing the following skipping sequence:

- A single bounce.
- As the lineman jumps forward with his right foot, he should extend his left leg backward, while bending forward slightly at the waist.
- Kick forward with his left foot landing in the spot vacated by his right foot.
- As the lineman kicks forward with his left foot; extend his right leg forward above the floor, lean backward with his head and shoulder.
- Kick backward with his right foot landing in the spot vacated by his left foot; extend his left leg backward, bending forward slightly at the waist.

Coaching Point:

- The emphasis should be upon intense concentration, precision of movement, timing, and developing a high degree of the motor skills involved in skipping rope.

DRILL #19: ROPE SKIPPING - HEEL AND TOE

Objective: To develop footwork, coordination, and balance.

Equipment Needed: Jump rope.

Description: The drill involves having the lineman skip rope, while performing the following skipping sequence:

- A single bounce.
- Touch his right heel out in front as he does a left-foot bounce.
- Touch his right toe in back as he does a left foot-bounce.
- To change to his left foot, from the right-toe touching position, he shifts his weight and jumps to a one-foot position, landing on the ball of his right foot as his left toe is touched back.
- Touch his left heel out in front as he does a right-foot bounce.
- Touch his left toe in back as he does a right-foot bounce.
- Reverse the previous procedure when changing back to the other foot.

Coaching Point:

- The emphasis should be upon intense concentration, precision of movement, timing, and developing a high degree of the motor skills involved in skipping rope.

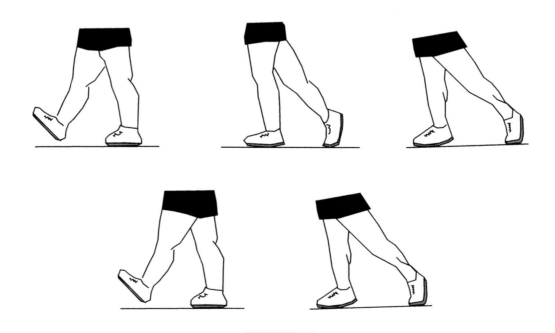

DRILL #20: ROPE SKIPPING – STOMP

Objective: To develop footwork, coordination, and balance.

Equipment Needed: Jump rope.

Description: The drill involves having the lineman skip rope, while performing the following skipping sequence:

- A single bounce.
- Touch the floor out in front with his right heel as he bounces on his left foot (the heel is touched simultaneously with the bounce of the left foot).
- Touch his left heel out in front as he does a right-foot bounce.

Coaching Point:

- The emphasis should be upon intense concentration, precision of movement, timing, and developing a high degree of the motor skills involved in skipping rope.

CHAPTER 2

AGILITY DRILLS

DRILL #21: RUNNING ROPES — EVERY HOLE

Objective: To teach high-knee action; to enhance the ability to move quickly and be light on the feet.

Equipment Needed: One set of running ropes.

Description: Players line up in a single line, and, on command, run through the ropes hitting each hole.

Coaching Points:

*   Players should develop confidence in their ability to keep their eyes up and not have to look down while running.
*   When performing the drill, the players should carry their hands up, similar to the position in which they're held in pass protection.

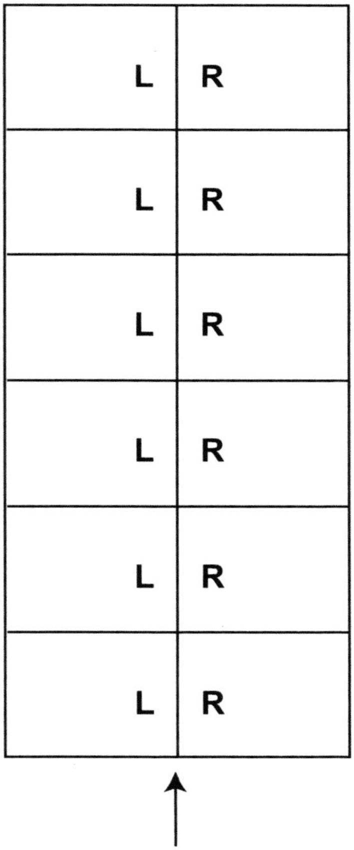

L	R
L	R
L	R
L	R
L	R
L	R

↑

DRILL #22: RUNNING ROPES — EVERY OTHER HOLE

Objective: To teach high-knee action; to enhance the ability to move quickly and be light on the feet.

Equipment Needed: One set of running ropes.

Description: Players line up in a single line, and, on command, run through the ropes hitting every other hole.

Coaching Points:

- Players should develop confidence in their ability to keep their eyes up and not have to look down while running.
- When performing the drill, the players should carry their hands up, similar to the position in which they're held in pass protection.

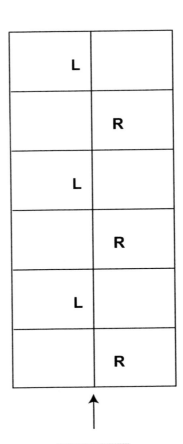

DRILL #23: RUNNING ROPES — SWIVEL HIPS

Objective: To teach high-knee action; to enhance the ability to move quickly and be light on the feet.

Equipment Needed: One set of running ropes.

Description: Players line up in a single line, and, on command, run through the ropes hitting every other hole opposite the stepping foot.

Coaching Points:

- Players should develop confidence in their ability to keep their eyes up and not have to look down while running.
- When performing the drill, the players should carry their hands up, similar to the position in which they're held in pass protection.
- The players should begin this drill slowly and gain speed as they gain confidence in their ability to perform the drill properly.
- Each player should strive to keep his hips over the middle rope.

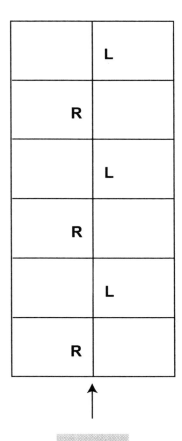

DRILL #24: RUNNING ROPES — IN AND OUT

Objective: To teach high-knee action; to enhance the ability to move quickly and be light on the feet.

Equipment Needed: One set of running ropes.

Description: Players line up to the side of the first hole, and, on command, run through the ropes hitting every other hole while crisscrossing the set. The third set of steps should be outside the ropes.

Coaching Points:

- Players should develop confidence in their ability to keep their eyes up and not have to look down while running.
- When performing the drill, the players should carry their hands up, similar to the position in which they're held in pass protection.

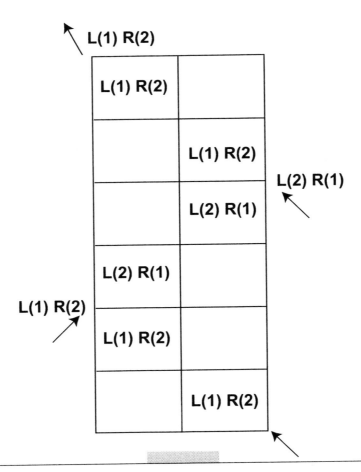

DRILL #25: RUNNING ROPES – SHUFFLE

Objective: To teach high-knee action; to enhance the ability to move quickly and be light on the feet.

Equipment Needed: One set of running ropes.

Description: Players line up to the side of the first hole facing to the side, and, on command, run through the ropes, moving straight down one side of the set.

Coaching Points:

- Players should develop confidence in their ability to keep their eyes up and not have to look down while running.
- When performing the drill, the players should carry their hands up, similar to the position in which they're held in pass protection.
- The coach should make sure to work players both ways so that each man gets to work both to his right and left.

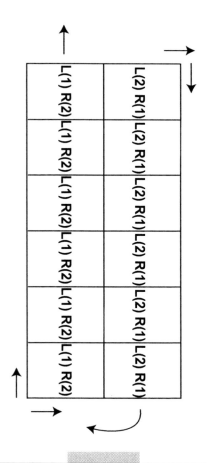

DRILL #26: 7-MAN SLED — SEAT ROLL

Objective: To teach the lineman to reset himself and to recoil and explode on movement.

Equipment Needed: A 7-man sled.

Description: The players line up in single file at one end of the seven-man sled. Upon command, the first offensive lineman in line strikes a blow and uses a seat roll to get to the next bag. He then hits every other bag down the sled. Once he strikes a blow and moves to the next bag to be hit, the next player in line starts the drill. When the first lineman finishes one trip down the line, he starts a new line on the opposite end of the sled. When all of the players have completed one trip down the sled to their right, the players then perform the drill in the opposite direction.

Coaching Point:

- The emphasis should be on quickness of movement and the lineman's ability to reset his body for the next explosive blow.

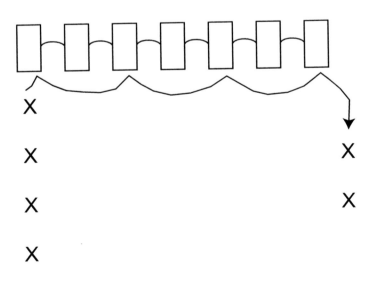

DRILL #27: SQUIRM

Objective: To develop body control and the ability to come off the ground quickly.

Equipment Needed: None.

Description: Players start in a 3-point stance and sprint five yards, at which point, the right hand goes down with all of the player's weight on it. The player then pivots 360 degrees, gets up and sprints five more yards, and then repeats the drill while grounding his left hand. After the left-handed spin, he then does a forward roll and comes up into a 5-yard sprint.

Coaching Point:

•   The emphasis should be on the player keeping his full weight on his hand.

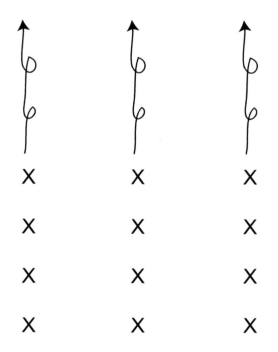

CHAPTER 3

RUN-BLOCKING
DRILLS

DRILL #28: DUCK WALK

Objective: To teach proper body demeanor, knee bend and weight distribution in coming off the ball.

Equipment Needed: None.

Description: The players are lined up straight across. On the snap count, they come off the ball with their back flat and their weight placed on the inside of their legs and feet.

Coaching Points:

- The players' initial steps and take-off should be watched closely to make sure that they are not overstriding.
- This is a great pre-practice, warm-up drill.
- The players should work going straight ahead, practicing with a lead step right and then a lead step left.

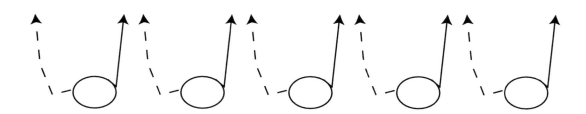

DRILL #29: BOARDS – FIT

Objective: To teach the blocker the proper fit into the defender on a drive block.

Equipment Needed: A board.

Description: The lineman fits into the defender with proper leverage, head placement, and knee bend. Upon the snap count, the lineman explodes his feet all the way through to the end of the board. The defender should give strong resistance.

Coaching Point:

- The coach should check the initial key elements to the block — a flat back, eyes up, proper leverage, and firing the feet and driving the hips through the block.

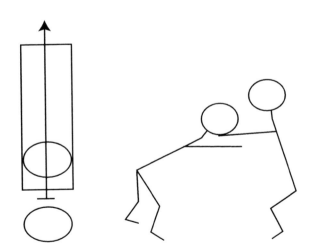

DRILL #30: TWO-STEP TO DRIVE

Objective: To teach the proper length of the first two steps and the arm pump.

Equipment Needed: A board.

Description: The lineman begins in a 2-point stance. The coach gives a command upon which the lineman quickly takes his first step and draws his elbows back. On the second command, the lineman quickly takes his second step, driving his fists to the proper landmark.

Coaching Points:

*   Each step should be approximately six inches long with the stagger foot going first.
*   The tips of the elbow should be drawn back tight to the body.
*   The coach should periodically have the blocker hold his position to double check whether he is in the proper fit.

DRILL #31: TWO-STEP FROM THE STANCE

Objective: To teach the proper quickness and length of the first two steps, the arm pump and the need to surge.

Equipment Needed: A board.

Description: The lineman begins from a 3-point stance. Upon the snap count, he fires off the L.O.S. for two steps, driving into defender.

Coaching Points:

- Each step should be approximately six inches long with the stagger foot going first.
- The tips of the elbow are drawn back tight to the body.
- The coach should periodically have the blocker hold his position to double check whether he is in the proper fit.
- Because of the desired shoulder surge into the block, the lineman may not be able to hold after his first two steps. Such an occurrence is acceptable.

DRILL #32: CHUTES AND BOARDS – DRIVE AND DOWN BLOCKS

Objective: To teach the blocker to stay low, gain distance and direction with each step, and maintain a good base.

Equipment Needed: Boards, chutes, 2-inch PVC pipe, shields (optional).

Description: The players line up in rows behind the chutes. On the snap count, the players explode off the ball and sprint through the chutes. On their second time through the chute, a defender is positioned in the chute, and the blocker drives him out. The players should concentrate on staying low and coming off together. Each end line works on a down block.

Coaching Points:

- The coach should check the players' stance, their ability to come off together, and stay low, and their step.
- The PVC pipe forces each blocker to gain distance and direction with each step without taking false steps or stepping underneath himself.

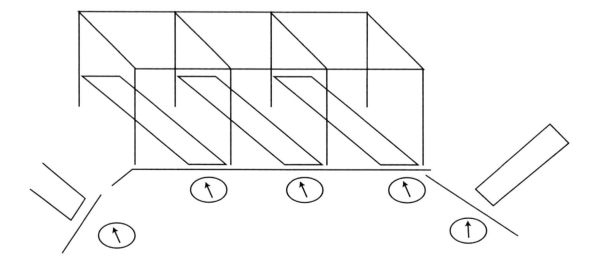

DRILL #33: CHUTES AND BOARDS — REACH/CUT-OFF BLOCKS

Objective: To teach the blocker to stay low, gain distance and direction with each step, and maintain a good base, all the while maintaining proper head placement.

Equipment Needed: Boards, chutes, 2-inch PVC pipe, shields (optional).

Description: The players line up in rows behind the chutes. On the snap count, the players whose left foot is aligned with the left bar in their section of the chute explode off the ball and sprint through the chutes. On their second time through the chutes, a defender is positioned in the chute, and the blocker reaches him and drives him out. The players should concentrate on staying low and coming off together.

Coaching Points:

- The coach should check the players' stance, their ability to come off together, and stay low, and their steps.
- The PVC pipe forces each blocker to gain distance and direction with each step without taking false steps or stepping underneath himself.

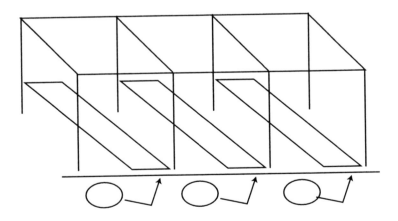

DRILL #34: REDIRECTION

Objective: To develop the ability of a blocker to react to a lost block or escape — react by redirecting himself in the proper direction to cut or occupy the defender by giving great effort.

Equipment Needed: Blocking dummies; boards.

Description: The blocker drives and knocks the defender who is holding a dummy off the board. Once he reaches the end of the board, the holder will run right or left at a 30-45 degree angle. As soon as blocker feels the loss of pressure, the blocker redirects his head, shoulders and body in that direction while trying to gain position on the far point of the dummy. The blocker just keeps accelerating in a low, two- or four-point blocking position.

Coaching Points:

- The blocker tries to stay on the defender or cut his legs and put the defender on the ground.
- One of the advantages of this drill is the fact that it involves an all-out effort.

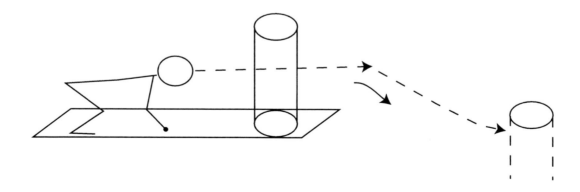

DRILL #35: CROSS FACE

Objective: To teach the blocker to fight and prevent the defender from crossing his face as the defender applies pressure to flatten the blocker and to attempt to work across his face for outside control.

Equipment Needed: None.

Description: The blocker assumes a shoulder-block position on the defender's outside number with his head. On the snap count, the blocker begins to take the defender off the L.O.S. by accelerating his outside leg upfield, pressing the defender to sustain leverage. The defender provides pressure to flatten the blocker out and to release across his face for outside control and containment.

Coaching Points:

- The blocker should have his feet up and under himself with a wide base and proper head placement.
- Two key principles that must be adhered to at all times during this drill are that the blocker must maintain frontal position with proper press, acceleration and body mechanics, and he must never be flattened out and lose position on the defender.

DRILL #36: BLAST

Objective: To develop the ability of the lineman to explode his hips; to teach the follow-through block.

Equipment Needed: Bags; shields.

Description: A blocking dummy is positioned horizontally and hand shields are laid on the ground behind the dummy. The defender lines up in a 2-point stance with both his heels touching the dummy. He can deliver a forearm shiver into the blocker but cannot turn or twist his body. The blocker explodes from his stance on the snap count and then drive blocks the man onto his back.

Coaching Points:

- The coach should check the blocker's leg drive and explosion.
- The blocker should target the base of the defender's numbers. A distance of five yards should be kept between the blocker and the defender.

DRILL #37: CUT SCRAMBLE

Objective: To teach the blocker to cutoff the forward charge of the defenders on the goal line; to teach a center's block on a shaded nose on sweep plays.

Equipment Needed: Boards; shields.

Description: The boards are positioned in a parallel design with the blocker on the opposite side of the board from the defender. On the snap count, the blocker crosses the board, placing his head across the defender reaching to the defender's far thigh pad. He then continues to run his feet, crabbing through the defender once his hands are grounded. The defender moves straight ahead and then gets width once contact is made.

Coaching Points:

- The coach should make sure the boards are placed far enough apart.
- The coach should check whether the blocker's head is up, the blocker's second step definitely gets over the board, and whether the blocker gives great effort to scramble through the defender.
- Some blockers will feel comfortable aligning close to the board and moving their first step over the board, while some will distance themselves from the board, take a short lead step, and drive their second step over the board.

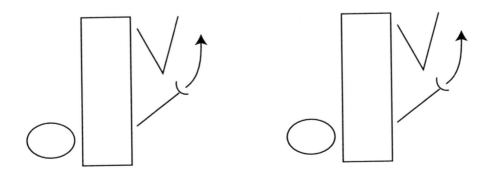

DRILL #38: STRETCH DRILL

Objective: To teach the blocker on outside zone or toss plays how to squeeze back into the defender and to get his hip past him to prevent pursuit to the ball.

Equipment Needed: None.

Description: Two players face the sideline, leaning into the other. On the whistle, both players work to get their inside hip past the other by ripping their near arm into the other and driving their inside foot downfield. This drill is designed to be very competitive, with one player being the right-side blocker and the other simulating the left-side blocker.

Coaching Points:

- Taking no false steps, using foot quickness with the inside foot driving down field, and maintaining proper leverage should be emphasized.
- This drill can be made very competitive with an emphasis on effort and finishing the block.

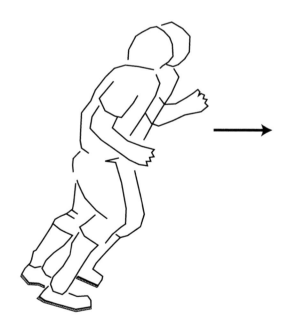

DRILL #39: PENDULUM SWING

Objective: To break down blocking into a simple progression and proper mechanics.

Equipment Needed: Two-man Rogers or Crowther sled.

Description: The player gets into a good football position slightly outside the pad (the point of his inside shoulder should be aligned in the center of the numbers). With his arm hanging at his side, he proceeds to step and strike a blow with his near forearm. The arm should move straight up parallel to his body and legs. The player should alternate his right and left arms, stepping with the near foot.

Coaching Point:

• Leading with the back of the hand should be stressed.

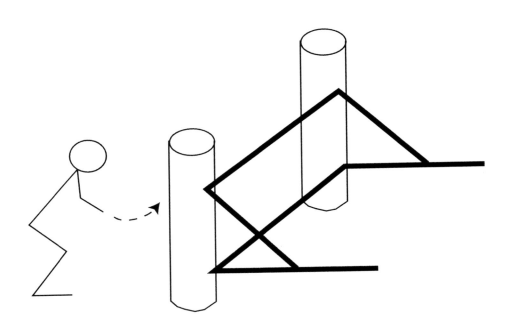

DRILL #40: TRIANGLE SWING

Objective: To break down blocking into a simple progression and proper mechanics.

Equipment Needed: Two-man Rogers or Crowther sled.

Description: A triangle is formed by the blocker's arm and shoulder. With his arm hanging limp at his side, he proceeds to step and strike a blow against the sled. In this instance, the blocker bends his arm at the elbow. As he bends at his elbow, his fist is positioned below his chin. He should lead with this triangle, exploding with it and providing a large blocking surface.

Coaching Points:

- The blocker's arm from his elbow to his shoulder should move straight up, parallel to his body and legs.
- The blocker should alternate his right and left arms with his near foot.

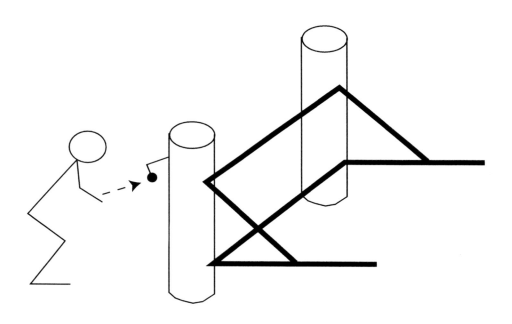

DRILL #41: 7-MAN SLED — 6-POINT EXPLOSION

Objective: To teach quickness of explosion; to develop the ability of the blocker to pull his hips through the block.

Equipment Needed: A 7-man sled.

Description: A lineman is positioned in front of each pad of the sled in a 6-point stance (i.e., on his knees, both hands grounded, and his toes curled underneath him). The coach then blows the whistle, and all seven players explode out into the sled, shooting the pads up and through the sled. They quickly recover and repeat the procedure two more times.

Coaching Points:

- It should be emphasized to the players that they must pull their hips through the block.
- When the drill is executed correctly, the player's pelvis and thighs should be the first to hit the ground.
- Players should be encouraged to move explosively.

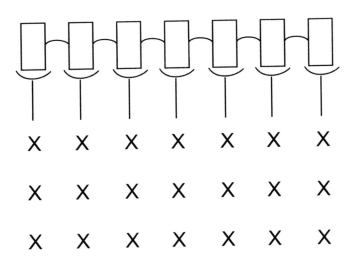

DRILL #42: TWO- AND SEVEN-MAN SLED

Objective: To develop proper explosion, an arched back and leg drive on the block.

Equipment Needed: A two- or a seven-man sled.

Description: The players line up in rows behind the pads on the sled. On the snap count, the players explode out and drive the sled for ten yards.

Coaching Point:

- The coach should check the players' stance, and whether their head is up, their hips shoot, and they have a wide base coming off together.

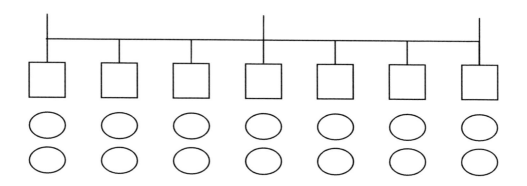

DRILL #43: 7-MAN SLED — REACH

Objective: To teach explosion, footwork, foot fire, and coming off the ball together.

Equipment Needed: A 7-man sled.

Description: The players form six lines, aligning in-between each pad. The coach then employs cadence and automatics to direct the line to reach block to either the right or the left.

Coaching Point:

- An explosive charge, a flat back, and proper head placement and foot movement should be stressed.

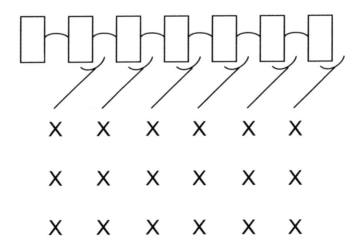

DRILL #44: BASE

Objective: To teach the players the importance of maintaining a good base.

Equipment Needed: Boards; shields (optional).

Description: The drill involves a defender who straddles the board with a shield (optional) and a blocker who attempts to drive him down and off the board. The offensive player goes when he is ready, and drives straight down the middle of the board. The defender plays the block.

Coaching Points:

- The coach should use a quick whistle, since the primary purpose of the drill is to focus on the base of each player.
- The teaching aspect of the drill can be enhanced by videotaping the blocker from behind performing the drill.

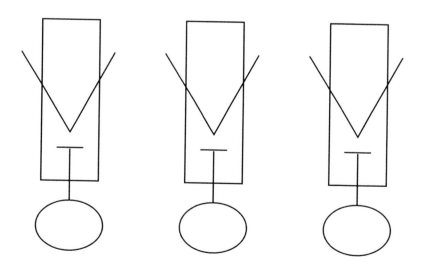

DRILL #45: CHUTE SCRIMMAGE

Objective: To teach and develop the basic fundamentals of a drive block.

Equipment Needed: A football; cones.

Description: Cones are used to lay the boundaries for a chute (lane). The players form groups of three. One group is on offense (a blocker, a quarterback, and a ball carrier). The other group is on defense (a tackler and two defenders who subsequently become the tackler). The drill involves the quarterback handing the ball to the running back who is following the drive block of the blocker. Essentially, the drill involves a one-on-one battle with only one snap per group. The defender aligns head up to the blocker and attempts to defeat his base block and tackle the ball carrier.

Coaching Points:

- This drill can be an exceptional tool for exposing all that is right or wrong with a simple drive block.
- The drill puts pressure on the blocker to perform. The entire team watches the drill, thereby putting the blocker in a position to "put up or shut up."
- The drill is designed to emphasize toughness.

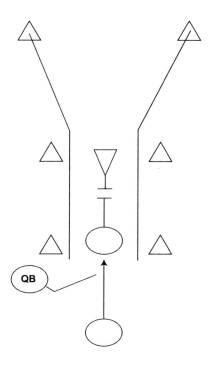

DRILL #46: WEAVE

Objective: To teach the drive blocker to keep pressure on the defender and to adjust as the defender tries to escape the block.

Equipment Needed: Shields.

Description: The players align locked up with a partner who is holding a shield tight against his body. On command, the blocker works the defender straight back. As the drill unfolds, the defender weaves from one side to the other.

Coaching Points:

- This drill forces the blocker to keep pressure on the defender while moving his feet to stay with the weaving movement of the defender.
- The blocker must maintain a good base throughout the drill.

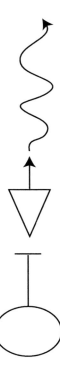

DRILL #47: FORCE AGAINST FORCE

Objective: To develop the ability to get off and maintain a good base.

Equipment Needed: One tall standing bag per two players.

Description: The players line up in a 3-point stance with a stand-up bag between them. On the snap count, both players come off the ball with one hitting the bag with his left shoulder, while the other hits the bag with his right shoulder. They should continue driving their feet through the block until a quick whistle.

Coaching Points:

- When the drill is executed properly by both players, the bag should rise straight up.
- A less-than-fundamentally-sound effort by either player would result in the bag spinning out of control.

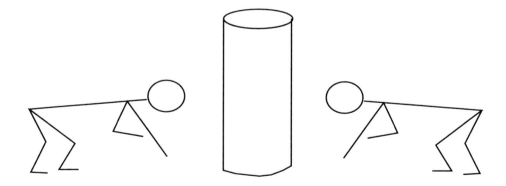

DRILL #48: TWO-MAN SLED – TRAP

Objective: To teach proper stance, footwork in the pull, explosion, and follow through.

Equipment Needed: A 2-man sled.

Description: The linemen line up facing out as indicated by the arrow on the diagram below. On the snap count, each player executes a short trap.

Coaching Point:

- The focus is on using proper footwork, not taking false steps, employing proper leverage on the sled, and exploding through the sled with a good base.

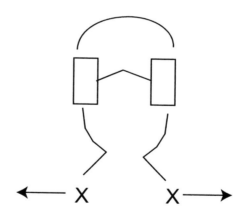

DRILL #49: TRAP REACTION

Objective: To teach the proper footwork and the correct reaction to various defensive schemes against the trap scheme.

Equipment Needed: Three shields.

Description: The linemen form a single line. The first three players in line, acting as defenders, hold a shield facing the line of blockers. The first blocker in line attacks the target (shield) chosen by the coach. On the snap signal, the coach designates the target by standing behind the shield to be blocked (i.e., he varies his position or remains stationary). The blocker attacks the near hip of the designated shield. To teach the blocker to react to a wrong-arm technique, the coach can have the defender in the #1 position attack the blocker attempting to come underneath the block.

Coaching Points:

- The coach should check for proper footwork with no false steps and that the blocker attacks the #1 position initially since this is the toughest block.
- Once the blocker attacks his initial target, he should react from that point on.
- A center can also be incorporated into the drill so that the guard gets a realistic feel for the block back and having to clear that block.

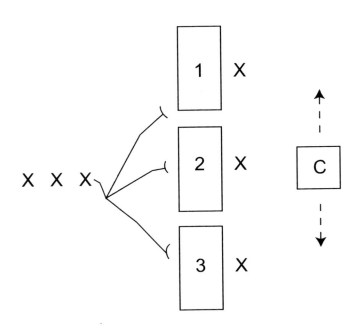

DRILL #50: REVERSE CROSS BODY

Objective: To teach the proper techniques of executing the reverse cross-body block.

Equipment Needed: Bags (optional).

Description: The drill involves having the blockers form four lines across from four defenders who are holding bags (optional). On command, the first blocker in line performs a reverse cross-body block against the defender across from him. The defender fights pressure of the block.

Coaching Points:

- In order to execute the reverse cross-body block properly, the lineman drives his head across the bag/body, driving his arm through the defender's knee and then working his hips around to pin the defender inside.
- Initially, the drill can be performed at half-speed so that the proper mechanics of the block can be practiced. Once those mechanics have been mastered, the drill can be performed at full speed.

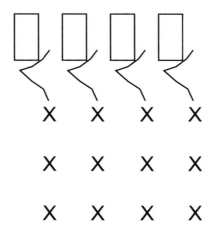

DRILL #51: PULLING AGAINST LINEBACKERS

Objective: To teach an offensive lineman the proper footwork coming out of a stance, how to keep his eyes on his assignment, and the proper technique for blocking a linebacker.

Equipment Needed: Four shields

Description: The offensive linemen form four lines. Holding shields, two defenders position themselves in front of the four lines, while two other defenders (acting as linebackers) line up as shown in the diagram below. On command, the first lineman in lines #1 and #3 pulls to block his assigned linebacker, while the first man in lines #2 and #4 executes a down block. Initially, the linebackers line up over the line assigned to block them. On the snap, they scrape over the top. Based on scouting-report information, the coach can tell the defenders how to react — whether flat or attacking downhill. The down linemen should fight the pressure of the down block as well.

Coaching Points:

- The coach should stand on the defensive side of the ball so he can see that the blocker's eyes never leave his assignment.
- Proper footwork, no false steps, and hitting through the linebacker with a good base should all be emphasized.

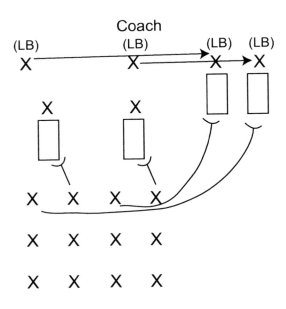

DRILL #52: COUNTER PULLING

Objective: To teach a lineman the technique of trapping and pulling to block a linebacker, while giving a second lineman who is pulling the correct relation between him and the trapper.

Equipment Needed: Four shields.

Description: The offensive linemen form four lines, Holding shields, two defenders position themselves in front of the four lines, while two other defenders — one acting as a linebacker and another as a defensive end — line up as shown in the diagram below. On command, the linemen who are first in lines #1 and #3 pull to block their assigned linebacker and defensive end respectively, while the first man in lines #2 and #4 executes down a block. Initially, the linebacker should line up over line #1. On the snap, he will scrape over the top. Based on scouting-report information, the coach can tell the defenders how to react, whether flat or attacking down hill. The defensive end should give different reactions as well. The down linemen should fight the pressure of the down block.

Coaching Points:

- If the trapper and the puller are side-by-side in a team's scheme, this drill should reflect that as well.
- The lineman pulling for the linebacker should be on the trapper's upfield hip.
- The trapper should work inside-out to kick-out, while the puller should keep his eyes on his linebacker.

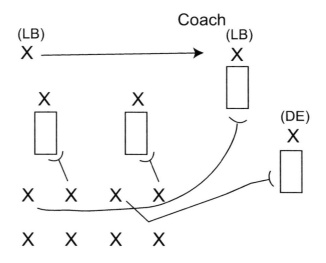

DRILL #53: DOUBLE TEAMS (POWER SCHEMES)

Objective: To teach the techniques involved in the double-team block in the power-off tackle scheme, working to the backside linebacker.

Equipment Needed: Three shields (optional).

Description: Two offensive linemen align with proper splits. Three defenders (a defensive end and two linebackers — a frontside linebacker and a backside linebacker) are positioned opposite the offensive linemen. The coach directs the defense to give different looks to the offense.

Coaching Points:

- A post block should not allow any penetration, incorporating all the elements of a good drive block.
- An offensive lineman must always protect from a run-through linebacker or a slanting lineman.
- The drive blocker should aim for the near hip of the defender, getting movement and swinging his hips to the post blocker, not allowing the defender to split the two.

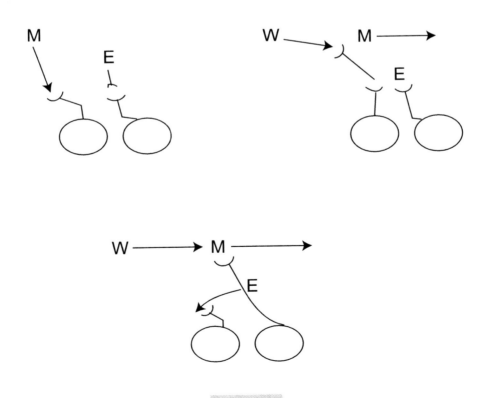

DRILL #54: COMBO DRILL

Objective: To teach offensive linemen in the inside-zone game how to get movement on a down lineman to the linebacker with appropriate reaction.

Equipment Needed: None.

Description: The drill involves two offensive linemen (blockers) and two defenders (one down defender and one linebacker). The linebacker is positioned at a depth of six yards, while the down defender is directly across from the two blockers. After good movement is made on the down defender, the coach directs the linebacker, forcing one lineman to overtake the down defender and one to work off to the linebacker.

Coaching Points:

*   The linemen work hip-to-hip and react.
*   The linemen should not be allowed to come off until they get movement.

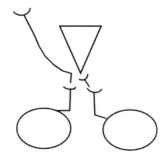
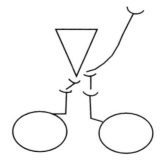

CHAPTER 4

PASS-PROTECTION DRILLS

DRILL #55: PASS SETS VERSUS A HEAD-UP DEFENDER

Objective: To build consistency in pass sets.

Equipment Needed: None.

Description: The drill involves three offensive linemen, a quarterback, and a defensive lineman. The defender aligns head up on the outside blocker. On command, the defender explodes to his pass rush lane. The offensive lineman takes his proper set and punches. A quick whistle allows the coach and the blocker to check the alignment between the launch point of the quarterback, the defender, and the blocker, and between the blocker and the defender.

Coaching Points: The blocker should:

- Take a 3″ lateral step inside with his inside foot.
- Focus his eyes on the inside V of the defender's neck.
- Keep his shoulders square.
- Keep the gate closed on either side.
- Make contact on the L.O.S.

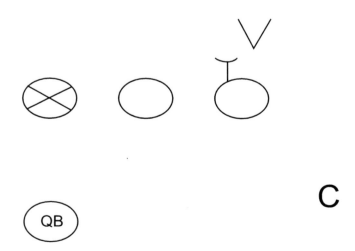

DRILL #56: PASS SETS VERSUS A DEFENDER INSIDE

Objective: To build consistency in pass sets.

Equipment Needed: None.

Description: The drill involves three offensive linemen, a quarterback, and a defensive lineman. The defender aligns inside. On command, the defender explodes to his pass-rush lane. The offensive lineman takes his proper set and punches. A quick whistle allows the coach and player to check the alignment between the launch point of the quarterback, the defender, and the blocker, and between the blocker and the defender.

Coaching Points: The blocker should:

*   Take a power step to the inside.
*   Focus his eyes on the inside V of the defender's neck.
*   Keep his shoulders square.
*   Keep the gate closed on either side.
*   Make contact on the L.O.S.

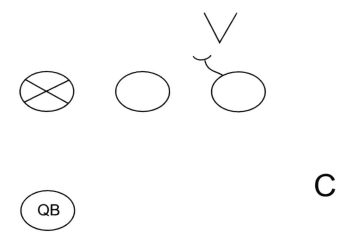

DRILL #57: PASS SETS VERSUS A DEFENDER ON THE LINEMAN'S OUTSIDE SHOULDER

Objective: To build consistency in pass sets.

Equipment Needed: None.

Description: The drill involves three offensive linemen, a quarterback, and a defensive lineman. The defender aligns inside. On command, the defender explodes to his pass-rush lane. The offensive lineman takes his proper set and punches. A quick whistle allows the coach and player to check the alignment between the launch point of the quarterback, the defender, and the blocker, and between the blocker and the defender.

Coaching Points: The blocker should:

*   Kick his outside foot to a stagger.
*   Focus his eyes on the inside V of the defender's neck.
*   Make contact on the L.O.S.
*   Against a wide rush, kick/slide to gain position in order to place the defender on his outside shoulder.

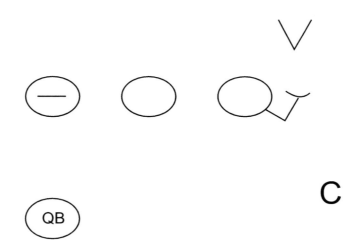

DRILL #58: BOOTLEG

Objective: To teach guards how to pull on bootlegs and how to react to various types of defensive end play.

Equipment Needed: A line spacer.

Description: The guard lines up on the line spacer. On the snap count, he pulls to block the opposite defensive end. The guard must know the launch point of the quarterback. If the quarterback is trying to break contain, the guard must take an approach to log the defensive end inside. If he is setting up behind the tackle, the guard can now work to kick the defensive end out.

Coaching Points:

- Proper pulling technique should be emphasized.
- The guard should be flat behind the center and gain depth after his fourth step and react according to the play of the defensive end.

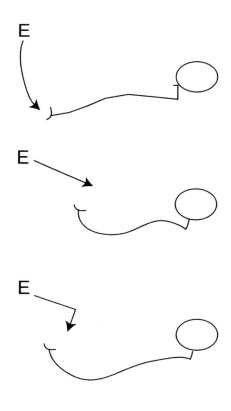

DRILL #59: PUNCH

Objective: To develop the fundamentals and techniques involved in the initial punch.

Equipment Needed: Sled (optional).

Description: The lineman aligns in a good pass set with the defender within striking distance. The lineman bends his knees for proper leverage on the defender. His elbows are in with his hands at chest level and with a slight bend in his arms. His shoulders are back with slight arch in his lower back. On the snap count, the lineman strikes up and out. Contact is made with the heel of his hands. His thumbs point upward with his hands forming a "W". His aiming point is the defender's pectorals.

Coaching Point:

*   Initially, the drill is conducted at a relatively slow speed and subsequently progresses to full speed.

DRILL #60: ENDURANCE PUNCHING HIGH-TO-LOW

Objective: To develop punching endurance, quickness, and the ability to adjust to different targets with a punch.

Equipment Needed: A hand shield.

Description: The partner holds a hand shield tightly against his body, while the lineman sets near the bag in a proper pass-set position. In 15-second spurts, the lineman punches the bag, switching from high-to-low aiming points on the bag.

Coaching Point:

- Hand placement, proper body alignment and knee bend should all be emphasized, as well as explosive punching.

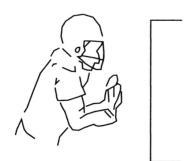
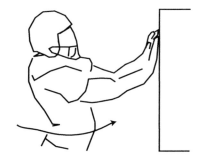

DRILL #61: ENDURANCE PUNCHING OPPOSITE CORNERS

Objective: To develop punching endurance, quickness, and the ability to adjust to different targets with a punch.

Equipment Needed: A hand shield.

Description: The partner holds a hand shield tightly against his body, while the lineman sets near the bag in a proper pass-set position. In 15-second spurts, the lineman punches the bag, switching from high-to-low, diagonally opposite aiming points on the bag.

Coaching Point:

- Hand placement, proper body alignment and knee bend should all be emphasized, as well as explosive punching.

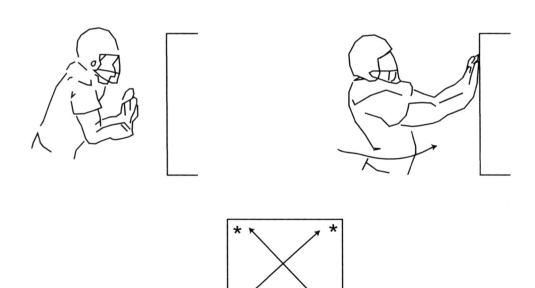

DRILL #62: ENDURANCE PUNCHING FOUR CORNERS

Objective: To develop punching endurance, quickness, and the ability to adjust to different targets with a punch.

Equipment Needed: A hand shield.

Description: The partner holds a hand shield tightly against his body, while the lineman sets near the bag in a proper pass-set position. In 15-second spurts, the lineman punches the bag, subsequently striking the four corner aiming points on the bag.

Coaching Point:

- Hand placement, proper body alignment and knee bend should all be emphasized, as well as explosive punching.

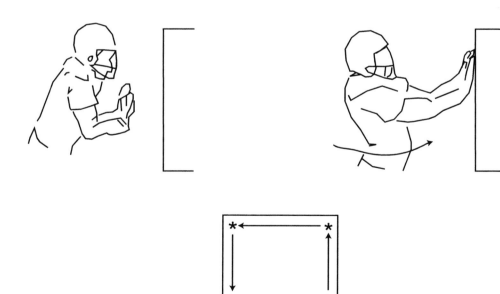

DRILL #63: MIRROR PUNCH

Objective: To develop footwork, coordination, and punch fundamentals.

Equipment Needed: None.

Description: The lineman begins the drill in a proper pass-protection, two-point stance. The partner aligns head-up within the strike zone. The partner initiates the drill by stepping to his right or left. The lineman reacts and mirrors the foot movement, while punching with his corresponding hand. The defender varies his movement, thereby forcing the lineman to react and punch. The drill is continued for approximately 10 seconds.

Coaching Point:

- Both elements of a proper pass block by an offensive lineman must come together — blocking the defender with his feet and matching the defender's upper body with his.

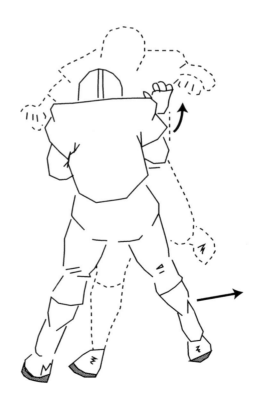

DRILL #64: LEAN

Objective: To develop the tight hands, timing and techniques involved in punching.

Equipment Needed: None.

Description: The lineman begins in his proper 2-point, pass-protection stance. The defender aligns perpendicular to the lineman, slightly further from the lineman's strike zone. The drill begins with the defender leaning into the strike zone. The offensive player reacts with a strong punch that is designed to knock the defender back to his initial place. The defender then moves down the line forcing the lineman to shuffle and maintain his base, while recoiling from his punch.

Coaching Point:

* The target should be narrow enough to force proper hand placement, while focusing on the target and throwing a tight punch.

DRILL #65: SHUFFLE/PUNCH

Objective: To practice the kick shuffle; to develop the fundamentals and techniques involved in punching.

Equipment Needed: A five- or seven-man sled.

Description: The lineman aligns square to the first pad of a sled in a good pass- protection set. On the snap count, the lineman power steps with his inside foot, shuffles square to the next pad, and delivers a good punch with each power step. The lineman continues the drill through the last pad. The left-side lineman and centers work left-to-right, while right-side personnel and centers work right-to- left.

Coaching Points:

*   While performing the drill, the lineman's knees should be bent, his hips should sink slightly with each punch, and his shoulders should be pressed back.
*   The lineman should maintain a good base throughout the drill.

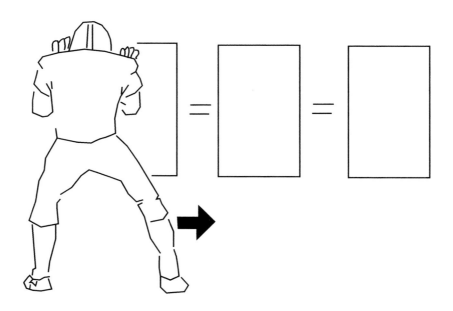

DRILL #66: SHUFFLE/PUNCH ON REACTION

Objective: To practice the kick shuffle; to develop the fundamentals and techniques involved in punching while reacting to movement.

Equipment Needed: A five- or seven-man sled.

Description: The lineman aligns square in the middle of the sled in a good pass-protection set. On the snap count, the lineman reacts to the hand motion of a coach and kicks his near foot, shuffling square to the next pad and delivers a good punch with each step. The lineman continues the drill for 5-6 changes in direction.

Coaching Points:

* While performing the drill, the lineman's knees should be bent, his hips should sink slightly with each punch, and his shoulders should be pressed back.
* The lineman should maintain a good base throughout the drill.

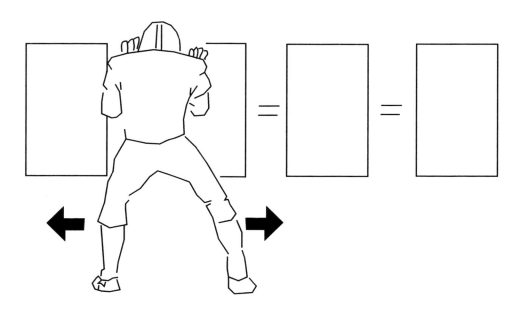

DRILL #67: BLOOD DRILL*

Objective: To develop timing and the ability to properly focus the punch.

Equipment Needed: None.

Description: Three defenders align in single file with the first pass rusher approximately 4-5 yards from an offensive lineman. On the snap count, the lineman, set at the L.O.S., strikes the initial rusher with a proper punch technique. Each rusher falls out following contact, and the lineman prepares for the next rusher. The rushers vary the speed and the type of rush they employ (e.g., bull, swim). The rusher may also stop short of the offensive lineman so that coach may make sure that the lineman is not lunging forward.

Coaching Point:

• Body position, punching technique and pulling the head out of each punch should be emphasized.

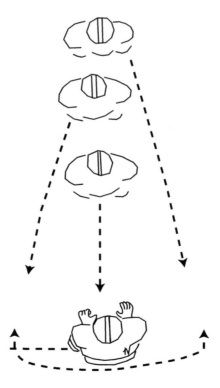

Note: The name of this drill originated with the author in 1975 because the drill was initially run without helmets, and when the drill is done improperly, it can result in bloody noses.

DRILL #68: HEAD SLAP

Objective: To emphasize upper body position in pass protection.

Equipment Needed: None.

Description: The drill involves an offensive lineman and a pass rusher. The lineman starts the drill in a 3-point stance. On the snap count, the lineman snaps to pass set. The rusher jumps into the lineman and attempts to slap the back of his helmet. The lineman then punches defender off and resets, retreating slightly after the punch.

Coaching Point:

- The lineman must keep his chin tucked, his head back, and his shoulders pulled back.

DRILL #69: HANDCUFFS

Objective: To develop the ability of the offensive lineman to keep his hands tight in pass protection.

Equipment Needed: A small bike tire tube.

Description: The bike tire tube is placed around the lineman's wrists in a figure-8 configuration. With his wrists bound by the tube, the lineman practices his pass set and various pass protection schemes against a defender. This procedure is designed to force the lineman to keep his hands tight.

Coaching Point:

• Body position and proper pass protection techniques should be emphasized.

DRILL #70: SPINNERS

Objective: To improve the ability of a lineman to execute the proper hand and extension action of pass protection versus a spinning pass rusher.

Equipment Needed: None.

Description: The lineman begins the drill in a proper stance. The defender aligns in any shade. On the snap count, the lineman explodes to a pass set and delivers a good initial punch against the defender, while the defender goes into a series of spin moves. The lineman must separate from the rusher and use his hands to maintain contact.

Coaching Points:

*   The coach should continually check for a fundamentally sound pass set.
*   The primary emphasis of the drill should be on the lineman not burying his head , getting arm extension, and moving his feet to maintain proper position in pass protection.

DRILL #71: HIT AND RECOIL

Objective: To teach the hit-and-recoil technique in pass protection versus a bull rush.

Equipment Needed: None.

Description: The defenders rush live. The offensive linemen are in a two-point stance. On the snap, the defender comes at the blocker. The lineman must set up, hit, and recoil. Against a bull rush, the blocker must sink his hips on the recoil and not lose leverage.

Coaching Points:

- The blocker should end up with his shoulders square to the quarterback.
- The blocker's stance, eye sight, exploding up and through, recoil, and mirror should be checked.
- The coach should observe the drill from different angles.

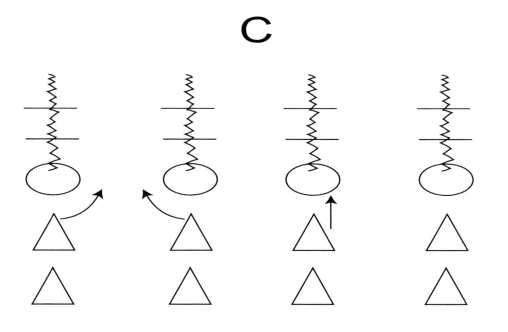

DRILL #72: HAND REPLACE

Objective: To teach the pass protector to constantly work to keep his hands inside on the chest of the rusher.

Equipment Needed: None.

Description: The offensive player assumes a proper position on the defender with his hands on the defender's chest. The defender proceeds to knock his hands off him in a variety of ways, for example, club up/down, grab the wrist, etc. The offensive player must get his hands back on the defender as quickly as possible.

Coaching Points:

- The drill should evolve to a point where the offensive player's eyes are closed so that he is forced to react by feel.
- The defender can turn his body to the side to force the blocker to put his hands tight on his shoulder as to not let him split his hands.

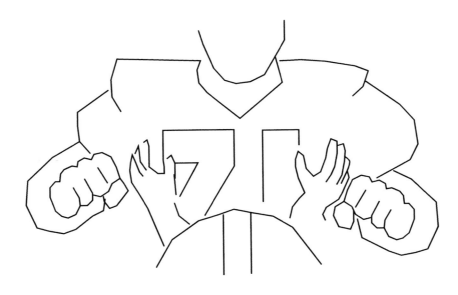

DRILL #73: INDEPENDENT PUNCHING

Objective: To improve the ability of a lineman to punch with both hands —independently of each other.

Equipment Needed: Two hand shields.

Description: The drill involves an offensive lineman and two defenders (each with a hand shield). The offensive lineman sets, and as he retreats, both of the defenders use the hand shields to "club" each shoulder of the lineman, attacking at different times. As they attack, the corresponding hand of the lineman punches out at the hand shield.

Coaching Points:

- The lineman must employ proper timing to punch out.
- The right hand of the lineman will not always be timed with his left.

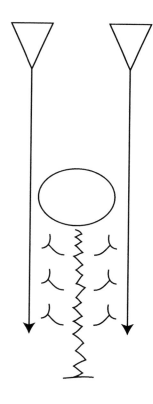

DRILL #74: CUT

Objective: To teach the cut technique on pass protection.

Equipment Needed: None.

Description: The defender plays live. On the snap count, the rusher attempts to go to the coach. The lineman must hit and recoil. After the first or second recoil, the rusher should be allowed to get as close as possible to the lineman. The lineman should fake with his arms and then cut him. The lineman should throw his thigh high and through the rusher, trying to keep on his hands and feet to scramble through him. If he should miss the rusher, he should leg whip him.

Coaching Points:

- The blocker's stance, eye sight, aiming point, and his ability to cut the rusher's legs should be checked.
- The coach should be sure that the blocker's hit and recoil are effective and that the blocker does not throw too early.
- The blocker should understand that the cut is a change-up technique.

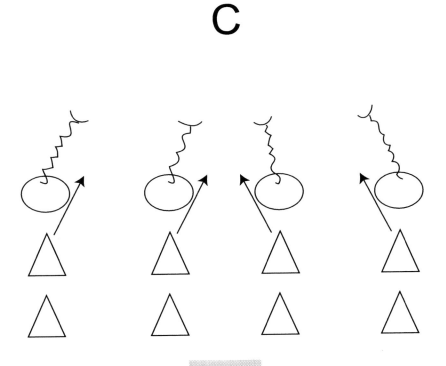

DRILL #75: LOVERS' LANE

Objective: To teach the 1-on-1 pass block.

Equipment Needed: Three large stand-up dummies.

Description: One stand-up dummy is positioned at the point from which the passer would throw. The other two dummies are laid on the ground approximately four yards apart. On the snap count, the blocker sets up, and the defender begins his pass rush. The drill continues until the defender reaches the stand up dummy.

Coaching Point:

- The need for the lineman to block the defender with his feet and match his upper body with the defender's should be emphasized.

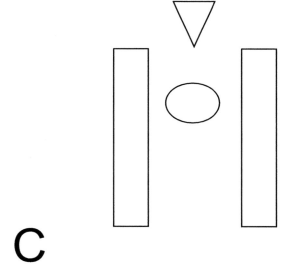

C

DRILL #76: TWIST

Objective: To teach linemen how to zone-off line twists.

Equipment Needed: None.

Description: This drill involves seven offensive linemen and seven defenders. The participants are positioned as shown in the diagram below. The coach works down the line directing the defenders as to the twist they should perform. Occasionally, the coach should require the defenders to perform a straight rush in order to not allow the offense to play the drill.

Coaching Points:

- Each lineman must learn to react to the defensive reaction.
- If his defender goes soft, the blocker should give some depth and attack in the direction the defender is twisting, physically bumping the next lineman off the penetrator.

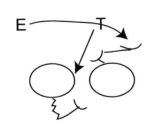
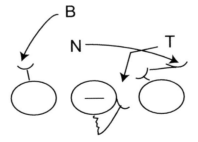
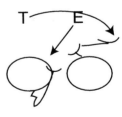

DRILL #77: BAG DRILLS — SHUFFLE

Objective: To develop the ability of a lineman to move while maintaining a proper football position and a good base as he steps over obstacles.

Equipment Needed: Five stand up bags.

Description: The players face straight ahead with the bags at their side. On the coach's command, each player shuffles straight down the line of bags stepping over each bag.

Coaching Points:

*   The player's weight should be distributed on the inside of the legs and feet.
*   At all times while performing this drill, the lineman should have a good base, with his knees bent, his shoulders erect, and his hands partially extended.
*   The lineman should never be allowed to cross his feet over.
*   The lineman should always lead with his near foot.

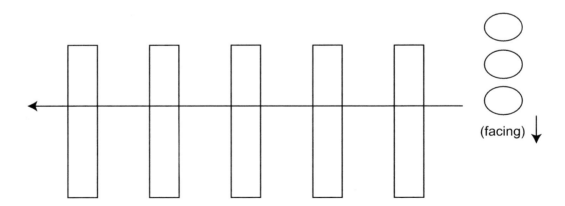

(facing)

DRILL #78: BAG DRILLS — HOP

Objective: To develop quick explosion with the legs.

Equipment Needed: Five stand up bags.

Description: The players align straight ahead facing the row of bags. On the coach's command, each player hops over the row of bags to the end.

Coaching Point:

• Having the lineman quickly explode up each time after hitting the ground on his hop should be emphasized.

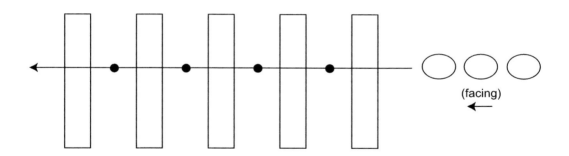

DRILL #79: BAG DRILLS — SIDE-TO-SIDE

Objective: To develop the ability to move, while maintaining a proper football position and a good base.

Equipment Needed: Five stand up bags.

Description: The players form a line facing the row of bags. On the coach's command, the first player in line moves sideways to his right. When he reaches the end of the bag, he sprints forward to the next aisle of bags. He then moves sideways down the aisle between the bags, sprints forward to the next aisle, etc., etc. Once the first lineman reaches the end of the first bag, the next lineman starts the drill. The drill continues until all of the linemen have performed the drill.

Coaching Points:

•   The lineman's weight should be distributed on the inside of his legs and feet.
•   At all times while performing the drill, the lineman should have a good base, with his knees bent, his shoulders erect, and his hands partially extended.

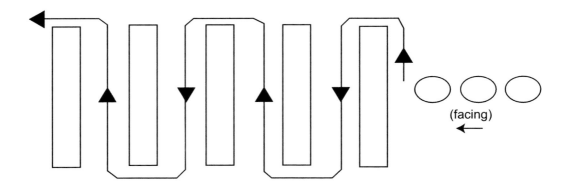

(facing)

DRILL #80: BAG DRILLS — FRONT TO BACK

Objective: To develop the ability to move, while maintaining a proper football position and a good base.

Equipment Needed: Five stand up bags.

Description: The players form a line with the bags to their side. On the coach's command, the first lineman in line sprints back and forth through the bags, keeping his shoulders square. When the lineman reaches the end of the first bag, the next player starts the drill.

Coaching Points:

- The lineman's weight should be distributed on the inside of his legs and feet.
- While performing the drill, the lineman should maintain a good base, with his knees bent, his shoulders erect, and his hands partially extended.

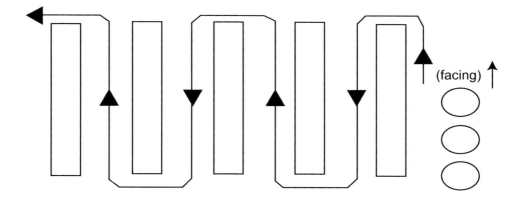

DRILL #81: BRACE

Objective: To emphasize the importance of the center of gravity and proper hip position in pass sets; to develop the lineman's ability to shift his weight against pressure.

Equipment Needed: None.

Description: The lineman begins the drill in a proper pass-set position with his hands behind his back. The defender hooks up under the shoulder pads of the lineman. On command (the snap count), the defender either pulls the lineman forward or pushes him back. The lineman must shift his hips to brace or anchor his center of gravity. The defender changes up his efforts, trying to destroy the lineman's balance. The drill is performed continuously for approximately ten seconds.

Coaching Points:

*   The lineman's shoulders should set back so a straight line could be drawn from his shoulders, down through the back of his knees to the balls of his feet.
*   The lineman should maintain a good knee bend.

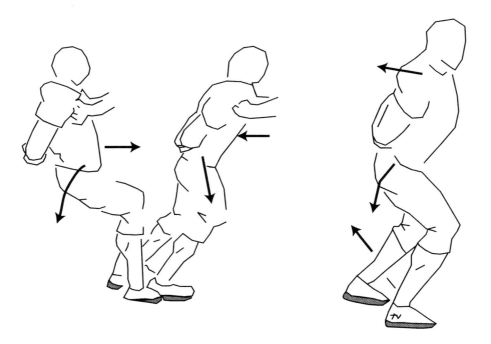

DRILL #82: PUSH PULL

Objective: To teach the proper way to defend against and block a defensive lineman who uses his hands to grab cloth and throw.

Equipment Needed: None.

Description: The blocker sets up. The defender grabs the blocker and attempts to turn his shoulders or pull the blocker forward. The blocker must use his arms to keep separation between the defensive man and himself. The blocker must squat down and drop his tail when the defender pulls him forward. As the blocker feels his shoulders being pulled, he needs to counter by extending his corresponding arm.

Coaching Points:

- The linemen should keep their feet moving while reacting to the push/pull efforts of the defender.
- This drill is excellent for developing balance.

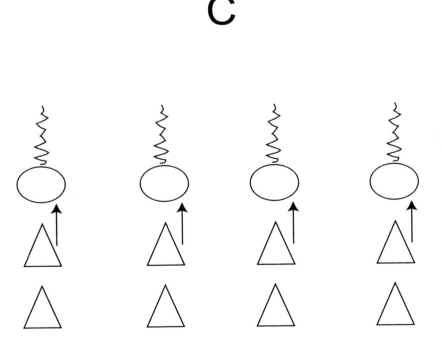

DRILL #83: PUSH PULL — RIP

Objective: To teach the proper way to defend against and block a defensive lineman who uses his hands to grab cloth and rip on pass rush.

Equipment Needed: None.

Description: The blocker sets up. The defender grabs the blocker and attempts to turn his shoulders or pull the blocker forward. The blocker must use his arms to keep separation between the defensive man and himself. The blocker must squat down and drop his tail when the defender pulls him forward. As the blocker feels his shoulders being pulled, he needs to counter by extending his corresponding arm. As the defender begins to rip, the blocker must move his feet and take his trail hand to flatten his hip out, not letting the defender clear his hip past the blocker's.

Coaching Points:

- The linemen should keep their feet moving while reacting to the push/pull and counter actions of the defender.
- This drill is excellent for developing balance.

C

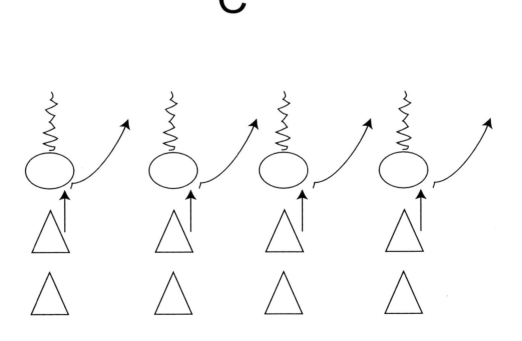

DRILL #84: PUSH PULL — SWIM

Objective: To teach the proper way to defend against and block a defensive lineman who uses his hands to grab cloth and swim on pass rush.

Equipment Needed: None.

Description: The blocker sets up. The defender grabs the blocker and either turns his shoulders or pulls him forward. The blocker must use his arms to keep separation between the defensive man and himself. The blocker must squat down and drop his tail when the defender pulls him forward. As the blocker feels his shoulder being pulled, he should counter by extending his corresponding arm. As the defender begins his swim move, the blocker must move his feet and take his trail hand to his arm pit, not permitting the defender to clear his shoulder past the blocker's.

Coaching Points:

- The linemen should keep their feet moving while reacting to the push/pull and counter efforts of the defenders.
- This drill is excellent for developing balance.

C

DRILL #85: ZIG ZAG

Objective: To develop a lineman's footwork off the L.O.S. and his ability to square his shoulders and maintain proper body position against a rusher.

Equipment Needed: None.

Description: The lineman begins the drill in a proper pass set with his hands behind his back. On the snap count, the defender moves toward the lineman, zig zagging up the field, while emphasizing lateral movement. The lineman sets off the ball, maintaining an inside position. He employs proper footwork to maintain that position.

Coaching Point:

- As needed, the lineman's alignment can be modified so that he can work on his footwork — particularly in the initial stages of his pass set.

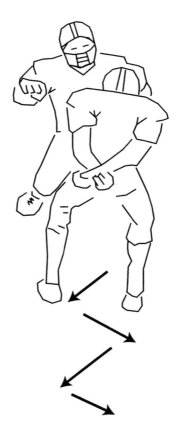

DRILL #86: MIRROR

Objective: To develop footwork; to improve a lineman's reaction skills.

Equipment Needed: Two cones.

Description: The lineman begins the drill in a two-point stance with his hands behind his back. The drill starts on the snap count. The defender works laterally between two cones that are set eight yards apart. The lineman mirrors the movement of the defender. The drill continues for approximately ten seconds.

Coaching Points:

- The emphasis should be on the lineman maintaining a good base.
- The lineman should focus on reacting quickly to all defensive movement.
- The lineman should maintain a proper weight distribution at all times during the drill.

DRILL #87: MIRROR DODGE

Objective: To improve a lineman's shuffle skills, punch action, and abiltiy to react quickly to rush moves.

Equipment Needed: Two cones.

Description: The lineman begins the drill in a proper stance. On the snap count, the lineman quickly assumes his pass set. The defender works laterally between the two cones which have been set approximately eight yards apart. The defender attempts to get the lineman leaning so that the defender can circle either cone. The lineman mirrors the movement of the defender, punching the rusher when he enters the "strike zone" (i.e., when the defender is close enough to the lineman to be hit if the lineman were to punch). The drill is continued for approximately ten seconds.

Coaching Points:

- The lineman should keep his shoulders square in order to prevent opening up a lane for the pass rusher to run through.
- The lineman should employ proper footwork in order to deny the defender access to his desired rushing lane.

DRILL #88: 2-MAN MIRROR DODGE

Objective: To improve a lineman's shuffle skills, punch action, and ability to react quickly to rush and twist moves.

Equipment Needed: Two cones.

Description: Two linemen begin the drill in their proper stance. On a snap count, the linemen snap to their pass set. The defenders constantly move side-to-side, occasionally twisting or spinning. Each lineman mirrors the movement of the defender across from him, punching the rusher when he enters the strike zone and passing him on to the adjacent lineman when handling the twist.

Coaching Points:

- The linemen should keep their shoulders square to prevent any defensive penetration.
- The linemen should employ proper footwork in order to deny the defender access to his desired rushing lane.

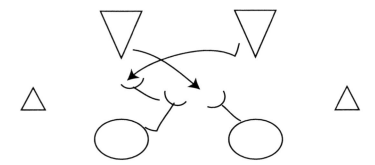

DRILL #89: DISADVANTAGE

Objective: To teach a pass protector how to recover after the defender has gotten by him and is now on the lineman's hip working to the quarterbaack.

Equipment Needed: None.

Description: The defender assumes a standing position perpendicular to the offensive lineman. The offensive player has his near hand ready to strike. The drill starts on the movement of the defender who attempts to pull himself through to the quarterback. The blocker reacts by stabbing his hand to the far breast of the defender and moving his feet in an attempt to get his off hand onto the chest of the defender.

Coaching Points:

- Sustained effort should be emphasized.
- The lineman should not step underneath himself.

_____ LOS

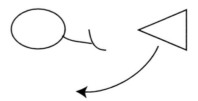

QB

CHAPTER 5

SUPPLEMENTAL DRILLS

DRILL #90: FUMBLE RECOVERY

Objective: To teach offensive linemen how to recover a fumble.

Equipment Needed: Two footballs.

Description: The drill involves having offensive linemen work in two groups on their blocking technique (for example, pulling to block a linebacker). Toward the end of their block, each of the two coaches involved in the drill drops a ball to the gound and calls out "ball". The lineman must then find the ball and recover the fumble.

Coaching Points:

*   In order to increase the number of repetitions that each lineman gets in the drill, two lines work away from each other.
*   When recovering a fumble, the lineman should fall to the side of the ball (not on top of it) and scoop the ball to his body, curling around it.
*   This drill should be performed at least once a week.

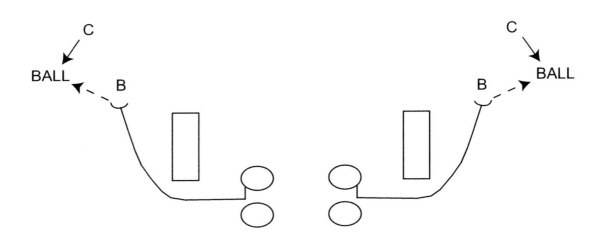

DRILL #91: TACKLING

Objective: To teach offensive linemen how to tackle in the open field following an interception.

Equipment Needed: None.

Description: The drill involves having two players (one serving as a tackler and one as the ball carrier) line up 12 yards apart. On command, the ball carrier attempts to get by the tackler. He runs full speed but is not permitted to run directly over the tackler. He can dodge, spin, stiff arm, etc. One of the best procedures to is have the ball carrier run directly to the tackler, execute a good head fake and then attempt to step away and score. The tackler should sprint and close the distance to 4-5 yards and begin to break down as he closes. Once the back makes his break, the tackler should step laterally, not forward. He should let the ball carrier come to him and then drive through him with a high chest tackle.

Coaching Points:

- The tackler's eyes should be focused on the ball carrier's midsection.
- The tackler should keep his feet driving until the ball carrier is down.
- In the open field, the tackle should be made higher in order to minimize the chance of missing the ball carrier.
- Tacklers should not leave their feet.

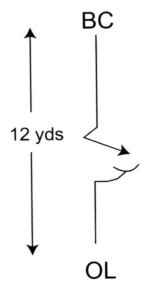

CHAPTER 6

TEAM AND GROUP DRILLS

DRILL #92: COMBINATION DRILL – INSIDE ZONE

Objective: To teach the proper execution of the inside-zone combination block between two linemen versus a down defender and a linebacker.

Equipment Needed: None.

Description: The drill involves two offensive linemen and two defenders, one serving as a down defender and one acting as a linebacker. The down defender is aligned over the outside blocker with the linebacker covering the inside blocker. The coach directs the defenders concerning what defensive reactions they should employ. In that regard, the coach places the emphasis on scouting tendencies to have the linemen work against what they will most likely see that particular week against the next opponent. The linemen react to the defenders' movements and execute a combination block.

Coaching Points:

- The lineman's aiming point should be the middle of the defender's playside number.
- The drill should emphasize reacting to the movement of the down lineman, denying penetration, stretching the defenders vertically, and staying square on the blocks.

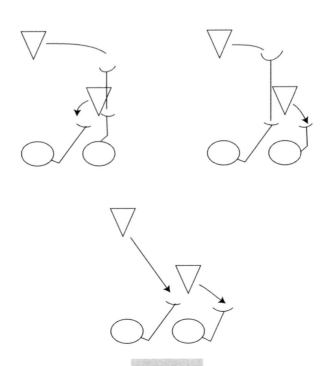

DRILL #93: COMBINATION DRILL — OUTSIDE ZONE

Objective: To teach the proper execution of the outside-zone combination block between two linemen versus a down defender and a linebacker.

Equipment Needed: None.

Description: The drill involves two offensive linemen and two defenders, one serving as a down lineman and one acting as a linebacker. The down defender is aligned over the outside blocker with the linebacker covering the inside blocker. The coach directs the defenders concerning what defensive reactions they should employ. In that regard, the coach places the emphasis on scouting tendencies to have the linemen work against what they will most likely see that particular week against the next opponent. The linemen should react to the defenders' movements and execute a combination block.

Coaching Points:

* The lineman's aiming point should be the arm pit of the down defender.
* The covered lineman should attempt to rip his inside arm through the down defender's arm pit.
* The covered lineman should work through to the second level and overtake the down lineman.

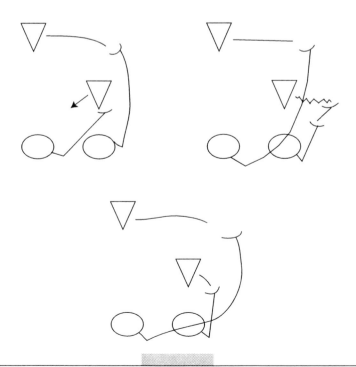

DRILL #94: KEY DRILL

Objective: To give offensive linemen practice utilizing various blocking schemes against defensive linemen.

Equipment Needed: Footballs.

Description: In order to get as many repetitions as possible, the drill is set up as diagrammed below. The quarterback takes the snap, and the running back gives flow one way or the other with the defense reacting. The coach calls the play, and the linemen execute the scheme.

Coaching Point:

• Assignments, footwork, head placement and executing of the called scheme should all be emphasized.

DRILL #95: HALF-LINE DRILL

Objective: To work on run plays to either the split side or the tight side.

Equipment Needed: Two footballs.

Description: The drill is set up for either the tight side or the split side. All plays are run to the designated side. The defense can use any defensive look they want. The offense executes the called blocking scheme.

Coaching Point:

* This drill is designed to help the linemen focus on their point of attack.

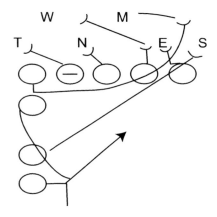

DRILL #96: INSIDE DRILL - RUN

Objective: To drill the offense on its inside runs versus the defensive front seven in the toughest possible situations.

Equipment Needed: A football.

Description: The offense aligns in its base formations and runs against any defensive front, utilizing running plays from off tackle to the split-side tackle. The offensive line executes the called blocking scheme.

Coaching Points:

- The emphasis of the drill is to employ base runs against base defensive looks.
- As a rule, the defense should not be permitted to incorporate an eighth defender in the drill.

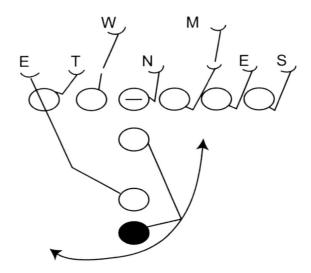

DRILL #97: ALIGNMENT AND ASSIGNMENT

Objective: To develop and practice the cohesion and timing involved in correctly blocking specific plays.

Equipment Needed: None.

Description: The drill involves two groups of blockers, with the first and second units behind the ball. The third unit is placed in defensive alignments. The coach calls the plays from the L.O.S. The blockers recognize and execute the desired blocking.

Coaching Points:

- The drill is not a walk-through but an up-tempo exercise.
- The coach should watch the linemen's fundamentals as well as their assignments.
- Even though the drill is conducted on a non-contact basis, it should be performed at full speed up to the point of contact so the coach can check for the linemen's head placement, footwork and assignment.

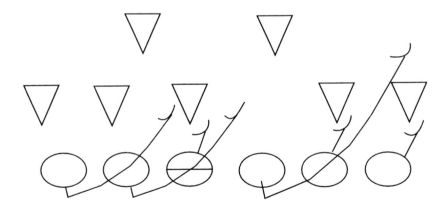

DRILL #98: HOOT 'N HOLLER

Objective: To develop a competitive spirit while executing the most basic of running plays — a straight dive.

Equipment Needed: Several cones; a football.

Description: In this drill, the offense is given three plays to move the ball 10 yards. The quarterback hands off on a straight dive to the left or right. The cones are set up at a width of 5-6 yards (depending on how tough the coach wants to make it for the offense).

Coaching Points:

- This drill is designed to work on basic fundamentals at all positions (e.g., coming off the ball with leverage, blocking with a solid base, moving the feet, etc.).
- Defenders can practice delivering a blow, shedding the block, and proper tackling.
- Toughness and competitiveness should be emphasized for all participants.

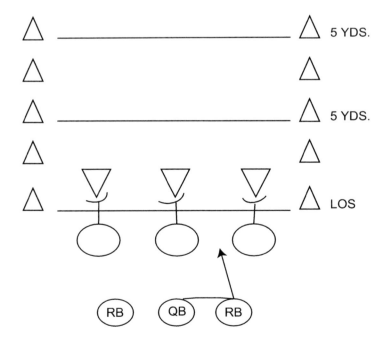

DRILL #99: BLITZ PICK UP

Objective: To give linemen practice on their protections; to improve the ability of linemen to pick up the possible blitzes of that week's opponent; to check the quarterback's understanding of any possible hot reads.

Equipment Needed: A football.

Description: The offense aligns in its base formations and runs protections that are utilized in the game plan. The period is scripted so that the coaches and players see the defensive stunts against various protections.

Coaching Points:

- Protections should not be employed and practiced that wouldn't be used against blitz.
- The coach should not build failure into the drill.
- The coach should give a quick whistle once the protection is set.

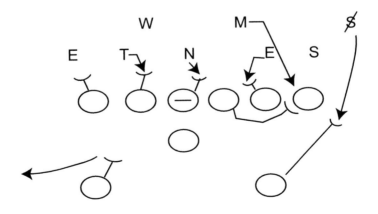

DRILL #100: GROUP PASS SETS

Objective: To teach the linemen the launch point of the quarterback for each protection and their desired body position on the defender they are responsible to block.

Equipment Needed: None.

Description: The coach should stand at the launch point for the called protection. The defense aligns and rushes their gap. The defender stops once he is fronted up by the protector. The offensive lineman then visually follows down the inside V of his neck until he is bending over, looking through his legs. If he has proper alignment on the defender, he should see the coach through his legs. If he has turned his shoulders too far or not far enough, he will be looking to either side of the coach. The drill should be conducted on a non-contact basis.

Coaching Point:

- This drill is a great exercise to use in pre-practice to check on the lineman's assignments and his footwork and to teach the lineman proper body positioning on the defender based on the called protection.

DRILL #101: COVER DRILL

Objective: To teach linemen to cover the football after it has been thrown.

Equipment Needed: A football.

Description: No defenders are used in this drill. The coach calls the protection and the snap count. On the snap, the linemen set in their pass protection. The coach then throws the ball to the right, the left or over the middle and calls, "ball". The linemen find the ball and then cover.

Coaching Point:

• In addition to teaching the lineman how to cover the ball on a pass play, another possible benefit of this drill is the fact that it can be used as a conditioning exercise.

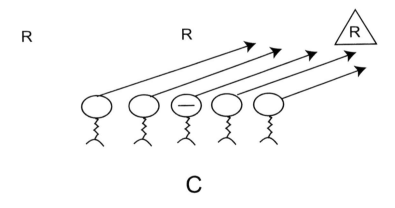

Steve Loney is offensive line coach for the Minnesota Vikings. Prior to accepting his present position in 2002, he served as the offensive coordinator and offensive line coach at Iowa State University for two seasons (2000-2001). Loney's success at Iowa State was reflected in the Cyclones' offensive units' high national standing since he returned to the Ames campus (he previously held the same position on the ISU staff for three seasons from 1995-97). The Cyclones were second in The Big 12 and 17th nationally in rushing yardage per game.

Prior to his position on the Cyclones' staff, he served for a pair of tremendously successful seasons in the same job at the University of Minnesota. Under Loney's guidance, the Gophers finished second in The Big Ten and 11th in the nation in rushing offense and averaged 415.4 offensive yards per game in his final season at Minnesota.

A 1974 graduate of Iowa State, Loney was a letterwinner on the offensive line for the Cyclones under head coach Johnny Majors. Loney began his coaching career in 1974 as a graduate assistant at his alma mater under head coach Earle Bruce. He then served as the offensive coordinator/offensive line coach at Missouri Western College in St. Joseph's, MO from 1975-76. Next, he accepted the job as head football coach at Leavenworth (KS) High School — a position he held for two seasons (1977-78). From 1979-83, he was on the staff at Morehead State in Morehead, KY, serving as the offensive coordinator/offensive line coach from 1978-80 and as the head coach from 1981-83.

In 1984, Loney left the Eagles' staff and went to The Citadel for three seasons (1984-86), where he served as the assistant head coach and tutored the offensive line and special teams. From 1989-92, he was the assistant head coach/offensive line coach under former Iowa State coach Earle Bruce at Colorado State. During his tenure at CSU, he helped lead the Rams to the school's first bowl appearance in 48 years. In 1993, he served as the assistant offensive line coach for the Arizona Cardinals of the NFL. Before joining the Cyclones' staff in 1995, he joined the staff at Connecticut for a season (1994) as the Huskies' assistant head coach/wide receiver coach.

Loney is widely respected as one of the outstanding young coaches in the game. Considered an exceptional teacher, Loney has coached a number of collegiate-level players who went on to play in the National Football League.